CREATING
FROM
SCRAP

BY LILLIAN and GODFREY FRANKEL

with drawings by **SHIZU**

STERLING PUBLISHING CO., INC. **NEW YORK**
Oak Tree Press Co., Ltd. London & Sydney

STERLING CRAFTS BOOKS

To

DANIEL JEREMY FRANKEL

who enjoys creating from scrap

Ninth Printing, 1973

Copyright © 1962 by Sterling Publishing Co., Inc.

419 Park Avenue South, New York, N.Y. 10016

British edition published by Oak Tree Press Co., Ltd., Nassau, Bahamas

Distributed in Australia and New Zealand by Oak Tree Press Co., Ltd.,

P.O. Box 34, Brickfield Hill, Sydney 2000, N.S.W.

Distributed in the United Kingdom and elsewhere in the British Commonwealth

by Ward Lock Ltd., 116 Baker Street, London W 1

Manufactured in the United States of America

All rights reserved

Library of Congress Catalog Card No.: 62–12593

ISBN 0–8069-5050–1   UK 7061 2306 9

5051–X

Contents

(Continued)

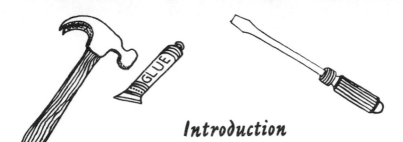

Introduction

If you have seemingly *useless* scraps and odds-and-ends around the house, you will be able to make *useful* objects from them by following the directions given in these pages. At the beginning of each article is a list of scrap and other materials that you will need. These are the ingredients for your project. Tools (such as hammer, screwdriver, frying pan, oilcan, etc.) are not listed in the ingredients because you probably have them around the house.

Read through all the directions before starting. Get your materials together. Then, when you do start, you will be able to complete your project without difficulty.

1.

Creating for Your Room

Burlap Rug

Scrap: large burlap sack
yarn

Here is a way to bring life to an old potato sack. Cut a piece about 24″ x 40″. Then unravel the edges for about 3″ so you have fringe all around. Do some overcast stitching where the fringe begins so the burlap will not unravel more than you want it to.

Now sketch out a design with a crayon. It can be an old-fashioned train, or a cowboy, or maybe an animal.

Then with yarn embroider your drawing. Do more than just an outline. Try to fill in the object with stitches, too, so that after a while your rug begins to take on another dimension. For some of the details you can do some painting, too. For example, if you are decorating your rug with a cowboy you may embroider the cowboy and horse, but paint in desert cactus, other horses in the background, the sun and a few clouds in the sky.

Pencil Holder

Scrap: small frozen juice can
colored string
Other materials: shellac
paste

Be sure the can has no sharp edges. Wipe paste or glue over the outside of the can. Wrap colored string or cord tightly around the can from top to bottom until it is entirely covered. Knot the end. Shellac over the string and let it dry.

Your colorful pencil holder will look fine on your desk.

Toy Storage Boxes

Scrap: bushel basket or apple crate
Other materials: nails
       glue
       rope
       enamel paint

Your room will always be neat if you make a storage box for your toys. Sandpaper the bushel basket, if that's what you're using, to remove the slivers. Then cover the basket inside and out with a coat of bright paint. Make the inside a different color, such as yellow outside and blue inside.

If you use an apple crate, remove the divider and keep only the outer frame. Reinforce the ends with new nails since apple crates are not nailed together too well. File or sandpaper rough edges and glue any shaky sections.

Drill two holes 4″ apart near the top of each end of the box. They are for the rope handles. Use a piece of rope about 12″ for each handle and make the knots on the inner side of the box. Paint your box with bright enamel and decorate it, after the paint is dry, with drawings of toys or favorite storybook characters.

Ball-Point Pen Holder

Scrap: corrugated cardboard
Other materials: poster paints
      ribbon scraps

Cut a strip of corrugated cardboard 2 feet long and 3 inches wide. All you have to do to make it into a Ball-Point Pen Holder is to roll it and pin the end. Now paint it with poster paint and tie several colored ribbons around it. You can now remove the pin, because the ribbon will hold the roll together. Stick in your pens and they will be handy when you need them.

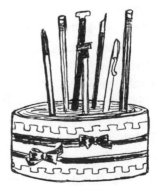

Spool Tie Rack

Scrap: board 18″ x 3″ x $\frac{3}{4}$″
        wire coat hanger
        8 empty spools
Other materials: varnish or paint
        small nails or screws

Saw the 18″ board into three pieces—one piece 12″ long and the two end pieces each 3″ long. Sandpaper each piece.

Measure 1″ from the end of each 3″ piece and drill a hole to hold the wire hanger. Nail or screw the 3″ pieces to the ends of the long piece. Untwist a wire coat hanger and cut off a 14″ straight section. Slide the spools over the wire, put the wire through the drilled holes and turn down the ends to keep it in place.

Paint your rack an attractive color or varnish it. Place a screw eye at each end of the back of the tie rack and hang it on hooks in your closet.

Matchbox Dresser

Scrap: empty penny matchboxes

wallpaper, oilcloth or fabric

If you are looking for a little container for your postage stamps, bobby pins or other small objects, you can make a matchbox dresser from left-over matchboxes.

First poke a round-headed metal paper fastener through the front of each little drawer to form a handle. Arrange the boxes in the design of furniture you prefer and glue them together.

Measure off a small piece of wallpaper, or oilcloth or fabric, and cut it to the correct size to cover the sides and top of the boxes. Paste it in place and then shellac it for a more durable finish.

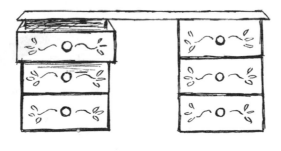

Jim-Dandy Jewelry Box

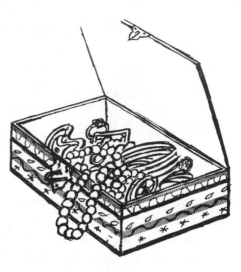

Scrap: wooden cigar box

wallpaper or color pictures from a magazine

Other materials: masking tape

paste

Cigar boxes are a very good size for a jewelry box. With a little decorating, you can turn one into something quite intriguing.

Select some wallpaper or magazine pictures. Place the box on the paper and draw around the box. Do this for all six sides—the bottom, top and the four sides, plus an extra piece for inside the lid. Cut out the paper. Place the paper on the surface you are covering, and with the masking tape, carefully paste down the edges.

Make drawings with brown or black crayon on the masking tape to resemble hinges and nailheads. Try to make it look like a treasure chest. Shellac your box so it will be more durable. If you want the box to be extra nice, line the inside with cloth.

Whatnot Box

Scrap: small wooden or tin box with lid
         cancelled stamps
Other materials: glue
         shellac

Have you a neat little box that you've been saving?
Why not fix it up for active use? Sandpaper the box
clean and smooth, if it's wooden, or wipe a metal box
clean.

Select a number of cancelled stamps of various colors.
Use foreign stamps too, if you have them. Place them
all over the top so that they overlap each other, and
glue them down carefully. If you have enough stamps,
decorate the sides too. Now shellac all over.

Now you have a handsome box for new stamps, paper
clips, thumb tacks and "whatnots." It will look fine on
any desk.

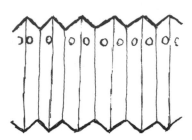 

Pleated Parchment Lamp Shade

Scrap: large piece of wrapping paper
          string, cord or ribbon
Other materials: linseed oil

You can make a very professional looking pleated parchment lamp shade to cover a shade that is faded or torn. Measure the lamp shade from top to bottom and measure the circumference around the bottom edge.

Cut a piece of heavy wrapping paper into a strip as high as the lamp shade and twice as long as the circumference. Now brush the paper with linseed oil. If you don't have a brush, use a ball of cotton. Let your paper dry for several days, and it will look like parchment.

Now with a ruler carefully measure off every inch, marking a dot at the top and bottom. But don't draw lines. In the middle of each space between the dots, punch a hole $\frac{3}{4}''$ from the edge of the paper. Use a paper punch for nice clean holes.

Place the edge of the ruler from top dot to bottom dot and fold the paper in a sharp crease. Continue folding, back and forth, until the paper resembles accordion pleats. Pull a thick string or cord through the holes and make a bow. You now have a new lamp shade!

Nail Keg Stool

Scrap: empty nail keg
burlap bag
$\frac{1}{2}$ yard of oilcloth
box crate
old pillow or foam rubber scraps
Other materials: 100 upholsterer's nails
100 tacks

When you finish putting these scraps together, you will have a really nice piece of furniture. Stand the keg, bottom side up, and wrap the burlap bag around it so that the burlap just reaches the bottom (closed end) of the keg. Tack the burlap to the keg around the top and bottom, and nail or sew the side seam. Turn the keg right side up and tuck the left-over burlap inside the barrel. A few tacks will hold it in place.

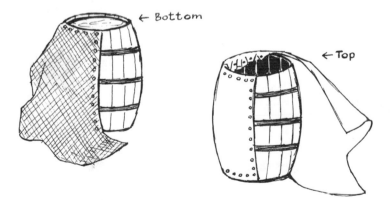

Cut strips of oilcloth long enough to go around the two ends of the barrel. Tack them down with uphol-

OIL CLOTH SEAT
OIL CLOTH STRIP

OIL CLOTH STRIP

sterer's nails and add more nails to form a design around the barrel. The picture may give you an idea.

You now need a seat for your stool. Take the two sturdy ends of an apple or orange crate and draw an $11\frac{1}{2}''$ circle on one and a $9''$ circle on the other. Carefully saw out these circles. Use an old pillow, pieces of quilt or foam rubber to pad the $11\frac{1}{2}''$ circle and cover it with a circle of oilcloth $18''$ in diameter. Place the oilcloth over the padding and nail the overlap to the underside of the wooden circle. You will have to make little pleats

SMALLER DISK

UPHOLSTERER'S NAILS

OIL CLOTH TUCKED UNDER

as you work because the oilcloth is larger than the seat. Now nail or screw the smaller circle to the bottom of the seat. That will keep the seat from slipping off the barrel. Your last step is to trim around the edge of the seat with upholsterer's nails.

Your Nail Keg Stool is now finished and ready for use. You can store some of your belongings inside the stool as a secret hiding place.

Book Ends

Scrap: 2 empty tin cans
wallpaper
Other materials: earth or sand
plants or rocks
glue, shellac

Use tin cans with smoothly removed tops. Discard the labels. Glue a magazine picture or a piece of wallpaper cut to size around the outside of the can. Then shellac over the decoration.

Place small plants and earth in each can. If your book ends will be in a rather dark place, with no sunlight, just fill each can halfway with sand. Then fill up the rest with pretty little rocks and white pebbles.

Either of these suggestions would make interesting book ends.

Decorated Wastebasket

Scrap: old wastebasket or empty can or carton
　　　　magazine covers or reproductions of paintings
Other materials: paste
　　　　shellac

You may have an old metal wastebasket that isn't pretty any more, or else you can use a large can or a small carton.

Clean it up and start looking for interesting pictures to decorate the basket. Perhaps you have some reproductions of famous paintings or funny magazine covers. Fit these pictures around the basket. You can cut them to fit, or overlap them any way you want. Then put paste on the basket and smooth the pictures into place. Shellac over the pictures to make them last.

Your basket will be a conversation piece.

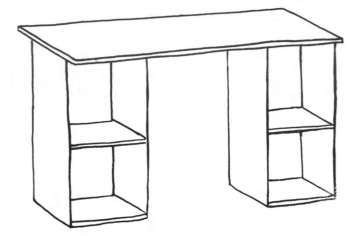

Kneehole Desk

Scrap: two orange crates
Other materials: large board or plywood
                   nails and screws

Ask for two sturdy orange crates at your neighborhood food store. Scrape off all the paper and sandpaper down the rough areas. Reinforce the middle shelf in each crate by gluing or nailing small blocks of wood underneath. If you want to conceal the blocks, fasten them way at the back.

Obtain a board or piece of plywood large enough to reach across both crates with enough space in the middle for your knees. Nail or screw the board to each crate.

Paint your desk, and after you fill the shelves with books and some of your other belongings, you will soon forget that your desk was once two orange crates. It will really be a piece of furniture.

2.
Gardening
Ideas

Easy Eggshell Planter

Scrap: eggshell halves
egg carton

Get a head start on gardening this year. Start your seedlings indoors in eggshells, while it is still cold outside. By the time it is warm enough for outdoor planting, your plants will be a good size.

Save up a dozen empty eggshells in an egg carton. Just save the larger part of the shells. Fill the shells with dirt, place a seed in each shell and cover with more dirt. Water daily.

After a few days, depending on the seed you planted, a little shoot will emerge. When your plant is several inches tall, the weather should be warm enough to plant your seedlings in the ground outside. Just poke a few holes in the bottom of the shells and plant them, eggshells and all! This is a quick and easy way to transplant seedlings without disturbing them. Try it!

Landscape in a Box

Scrap: cigar box
wallpaper and color picture
soil, stones, twigs
Other materials: plants
paste, string and toothpicks

Select a real-looking landscape painting from a magazine and paste it to the inside lid of a cigar box. Spread paste along the back of the paper hinge and hold the lid open till it sticks.

Cut wallpaper pieces to fit the outside of the box, sides and front, and paste them down smoothly. Place some tiny potted plants in the box. Fill the rest of the box with earth, interesting stones and small twigs. Plant a little grass seed in the earth. You can add seashells if you have any. Make a trellis or fence of string and toothpicks. This is your miniature garden landscape!

Seedling-Saver

Scrap: empty milk cartons

One of the best and easiest ways to protect new seedlings is by using a quart-size milk carton. Simply cut off the top and bottom of the carton and you will be left with the middle portion, open at both ends. Place the middle part over the seedling and press into the soil around the plant. Press it far enough down so that the wind won't blow the carton over. The opening at the top permits air and light to reach the seedling, but the carton affords protection from cold winds. When the seedling is sturdy, remove the Seedling-Saver.

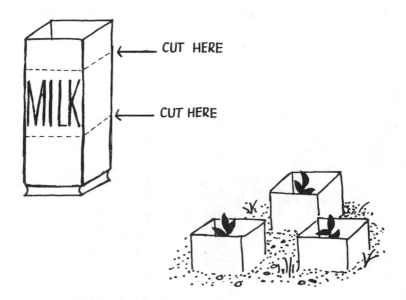

CUT HERE

CUT HERE

Muffin-Tin Garden

Scrap: old muffin tin
left-over seeds

An old muffin tin can become an attractive garden for your window sill. Put about $\frac{1}{4}''$ of fine gravel in each cup of the muffin tin. Then fill the cups with dirt, and plant different seeds in each one. Water the seeds daily. Thin out your seedlings so that just two plants are growing in each cup. You will have a little garden of a variety of plants for your window sill.

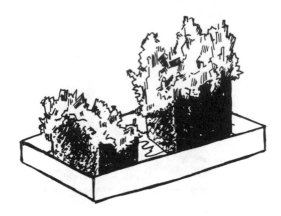

A Crystal Garden

Scrap: piece of brick
Other materials: salt
      liquid bluing
      household ammonia
      ink

Believe it or not, you can grow a pretty crystal garden on a piece of brick! Put it in a low dish—an old chipped one will do. Now mix 6 tablespoons each of salt, liquid bluing and household ammonia. Pour this mixture over the brick and put a few drops of blue or red ink into the dish. This will add color to the crystals when they begin to form.

In 15 or 20 minutes you will be able to notice little crystals forming all over the brick and around the rim of the dish. To keep your crystal garden blooming, just add a teaspoon of ammonia every week. See how long you can keep your garden growing.

3.
Creating
Things
for the
House

Shoe Scraper

Scrap: 75 or more metal bottle caps
      plywood about 16″ x 16″
Other materials: 75 or more ¾″ nails

With this shoe scraper you should be able to keep mud and snow out of the house.

If you use a board 16″ x 16″ you will need at least 75 bottle caps. Place them side by side and upside down on your board. Place all the rows close together so that the caps almost touch each other.

Hammer each cap to the board with a nail. Be sure each cap is secure and does not move. Use the Shoe Scraper in the garage, or outside of the door to your house. When too much snow or mud gets packed into the scraper, turn it over and hit it on the ground several times. If there is wet mud on it you may have to wait for it to dry before it will fall off readily.

Fruit Bowl

Scrap: old scratched breakable record

Do you have an old breakable phonograph record that is too scratched to play any more? You can convert it into a fruit bowl!

Heat the kitchen oven to 350 degrees. Place the record in the oven for 10 minutes. Then open the oven and with a pair of pliers or tongs take out the record and try to bend it. If it isn't pliable, put it back in the oven a little while longer. Don't touch the record with your bare hands.

Test the record again in a little while. If it bends easily take it out and try to bend it with the pliers into a bowl. Work it until you have the shape you want. You will be able to handle it soon after you take it out of the oven. Once you have molded it into a suitable bowl let it cool and harden.

If you change your mind about the shape after it has cooled you'll have to reheat it. When it's just right in shape, paint your bowl with enamel or poster paints. Use broad bold strokes to cover all the surfaces. You can add designs to your bowl to give it an extra special artistic appearance. But don't expect it to last very long!

Tool Hanger

Scrap: empty spools
            long nails
Other materials: board 20" long

A handy and safe way to keep your tools is to hang them up out of everyone's way. Here is a simple Tool Hanger you can make with empty spools and a piece of wood.

Find a board and cut it down to about 20" long. You will hang it horizontally. Decide what you will want to hang up, for that will determine how you will space the spools. To hang up a hammer you need two spools rather close together. The spools can be farther apart for a rake. Mark off with a pencil where you want to place your spools. Then hammer a nail through each spool opening into the board. That is why the nail should be longer than the spool.

Nail or screw the hanger to the garage or basement wall.

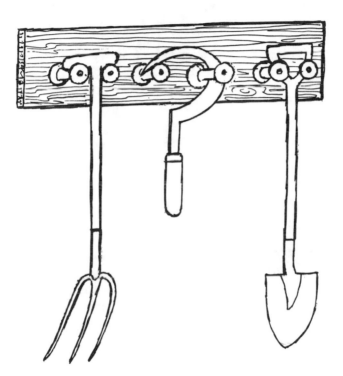

Knife Holder

Scrap: cardboard cigar box
      wallpaper
Other materials: glue and base molding

The safest place to keep sharp knives is in a Knife Holder. You can make one out of a cigar box. Open the box and glue small pieces of base molding in each corner to reinforce the box. They should be as deep as the box.

At one end of the box cut three or four slots $1\frac{1}{2}''$ apart for the knives. Now glue down the lid. Select a decorative piece of wallpaper from your scrap collection and paste it neatly around the box.

To hang the Knife Holder, place screw eyes at the top corners and hang it on the wall.

Hot Plate

Scrap: 19 cardboard milk bottle tops
odds and ends of yarn

Save 19 cardboard milk tops. Wash them and let them dry. Thread a large needle with colorful yarn and poke the needle through the center of a bottle top. Pull the yarn through. Sew through the hole in the center and around to the back of the bottle top and through the center again as shown in the drawing. Leave just a tiny space between the strands. When you finish, carefully tie a knot so it won't unravel. Vary the colors of the different bottle tops. Cover some red, others green, yellow, and so on.

When you have covered all the bottle tops with yarn, sew them together into a mat. Let the tops overlap each other. You can make a circular mat as in the drawing. If you make a square one, you will need a different number of bottle tops, depending upon the size of your mat.

Bottle-Cap Hot Plates

Scrap: 64 pop bottle caps
8" square of plywood

Other materials: glue and paint

Trim and sandpaper your piece of wood until it is smooth, especially around the edges. Arrange the bottle caps with their tops up on the sheet of wood. Glue them to the wood and when the glue is dry, paint the entire board and caps with enamel and you will have a nice hot plate.

You can make another hot plate by arranging your bottle caps into a design. For instance, a bunch of grapes would make a clever arrangement. Then you could paint the grapes purple and paint leaves and vines in green on the wood.

This is a good object to make for your mother or grandmother.

Still-Life Place Mats

Scrap: old sheet
        newspapers
Other materials: crayons
        paper towels

Cut an old sheet into rectangles about 15″ x 20″. Unravel threads around the edges of each place mat until you have a $\frac{1}{2}$″ fringe on each side. Now your mats are almost ready for decorating, but you will find it easier to draw on cloth that is stiff. Starch your mats with laundry starch so that they are quite stiff when you iron them.

Decorate your place mats with crayons. Draw fruits, vegetables, flowers or leaves with bright colors. Next you must "set" your drawings so that they won't come off in the wash. To do this, place the mats face down on top of newspapers covered with paper towels, and iron them with a hot iron. Now your design will be lasting and will not come off.

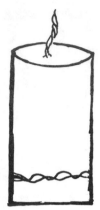

Decorative Candles

Scrap: bits of left-over crayons
      frozen juice can
      piece of string

You can make lovely little candles out of left-over scraps of crayons. First remove the paper wrappings. In a pan over low heat melt the crayons you want to use. Be sure it is all right to use the pan.

Do you remember how to mix colors?

While the crayons are melting, get a small gelatine mold or frozen juice can or any other small container with an interesting shape. Grease the insides with oil or margarine. Then cut some thick string into a piece the same length as the container. This will be the wick.

As soon as your wax mixture is soft enough pour it into the greased container while you dangle the piece of string down the middle of the container. When the wax reaches the top of the container hold onto the string for a minute or two. Allow the wax to cool and harden. When it is hard enough you can pull it out by gently tugging at the wick.

Little candles are nice to use as a centerpiece or to float in a small bowl along with water decorations.

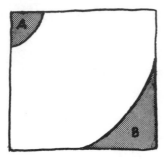

Hat-Stand

Scrap: cardboard or corrugated paper
Other materials: brads or glue

Your favorite hat or cap deserves a Hat-Stand all of its own. Cut a 12″ square of cardboard or corrugated paper. Cut off the corners as in the picture. With crayons, paints or magazine pictures decorate your Hat-Stand. Then when you have finished decorating it, fasten the straight edges together with several brads or glue. Stand it up in a corner of your dresser with your hat on it.

Napkin Rings

Scrap: cardboard cylinder from wax paper roll
        crepe paper or colored string
Other materials: paste, shellac

A cardboard cylinder is fine waste material for making napkin rings. Cut the roll into sections about $1\frac{1}{2}''$ wide.

Cut crepe paper crosswise into long strips $\frac{1}{2}''$ wide. Pull each strip until it resembles raffia. Paste one end inside the ring and proceed to wrap it around and around the ring until you have covered all the cardboard. Paste the last end on the inside so it won't show. If you have no crepe paper, you can use odds and ends of string.

Shellac the ring so it will have more permanence and a shiny surface. Make a different color for each member of your family. If you only have one color, make initials by rolling the crepe paper into a firm strip and gluing it onto the ring in the shape of letters. Then people can recognize their own Napkin Rings.

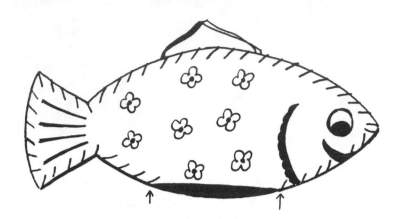

Fish Holder

Scrap: pieces of felt about 4″ x 7″

Draw a fish about 7″ long on a piece of paper. You can make him look real or funny. Put the two pieces of felt together and the pattern on top and cut out the fish shapes. Sew the two pieces of felt together with an overcast stitch all around the edge except for the part between the arrows. That is where you put your hand into the Fish Holder to hold a hot dish.

4.
Creating
Useful
Gadgets

Yarn Holder

Scrap: round oatmeal box
        magazine picture
Other materials: ball of yarn

This is a nice present to make for someone who knits.

Decorate an oatmeal box by pasting on colored magazine pictures or paper cut-outs. Then punch a small hole with a pencil about 3″ from the top of the box.

Put the ball of yarn into the box. From the inside, push one end of the yarn through the hole and close the box. When you pull the end of the yarn you won't have to worry about dropping the ball of yarn and unwinding it. It stays in place inside the box.

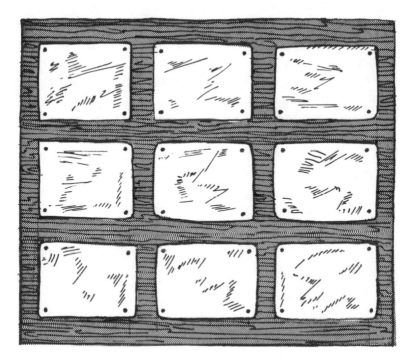

Light or Sun Reflector

Scrap: 9 TV dinner plates
Other materials: 24″ x 24″ piece of plywood
                 small nails

Here is a handy light reflector you can use in several ways. You can use it as an aid in getting tan when sun bathing or as a reflector for taking pictures.

First flatten nine rectangular tin-foil TV dinner plates. You can stamp them flat or use a hammer. It doesn't matter if the plates are somewhat wrinkled. As a matter of fact, this helps diffuse the light. Place the nine reflectors in three rows of 3 on the piece of plywood and hammer them to the board with a nail at each corner.

To use this convenient, lightweight reflector for photography, stand it so that it reflects light on your subject. For example, in an indoor picture set up the reflector near the window to catch and reflect light rays. If you're trying to get a nice suntan, prop the board up near you and it will reflect more sunlight on your body.

Decorative Door Stop

Scrap: brick
cloth or wallpaper
Other material: paste or glue

For a door that just won't stay open you can make a pretty door stop. All you need is a clean brick and some wallpaper, cloth or paint.

Place your brick on the material you are going to use to cover it and cut patterns for each side, allowing an extra $\frac{1}{2}''$ for each side to overlap. Paste or glue the pieces to the brick.

If you don't wish to cover the brick, you can paint it and then decorate it with strips of colored tape for a plaid effect.

Decorative Book Ends

Just make two door stops and you will have a nice pair of book ends!

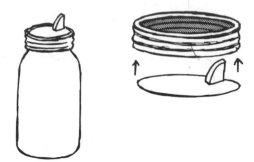

Fire Extinguisher

Scrap: 1-quart mason jar with metal ring
empty salt box with pouring spout
Other materials: 1 pint of sawdust
1 pint of bicarbonate of soda

Make your home safer with a handy fire extinguisher. Find a canning jar with a two-part metal lid. You will need the hollow ring part.

Cut the top off of a salt box with a tin pouring spout. Cut it so it is just the right size to fit securely inside the metal ring.

Mix together 1 pint of sawdust (which you can get from a lumber yard) and a pint of dry bicarbonate of soda. Pour them into the jar. Screw on the metal band with its pouring spout lid and your fire extinguisher is ready for use. Check to be sure that the spout opens easily.

5.
Creating Things for Outdoors

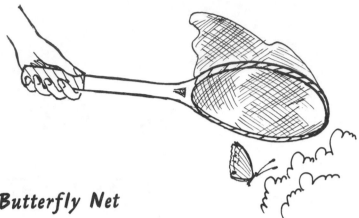

Butterfly Net

Scrap: old tennis racket frame
old sheet
mosquito netting

Pull out the gut from an unused tennis racket. Cut a strip of muslin about 3″ wide and 5′ long from an old sheet. Wrap it tightly around the rim of the racket, overlapping the edges, and stitch down the end so it stays nice and tight.

Fold a piece of mosquito netting about 24″ by 36″ in half and stitch it into a rounded bag. You don't want any corners because it is hard to get butterflies out of corners. Stitch the top of the bag to the muslin around the frame and your butterfly net is ready for action.

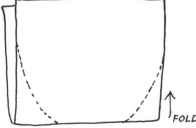

FOLD

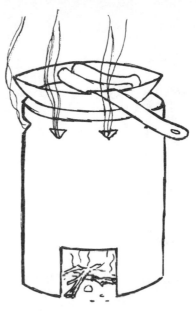

Camp Stove

Scrap: #10 tin can

A large tin can, preferably a #10 size, will make a very useful camp stove. At the open end of the can cut away a 3″ x 3″ section with tin snips. This will be the bottom of your stove. Then turn the can over and poke several holes around the top just below the rim, using a juice can opener or an ice pick.

To use your Camp Stove, build a little fire under it. You can take care of the fire in the 3″ opening. Place your food, such as meat or an egg, directly on the flat top of the stove (with a little grease to keep it from sticking). Or else you can use a frying pan on top of the stove. You will enjoy your camp supper!

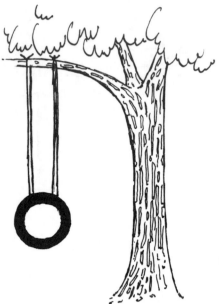

Outdoor Swing

Scrap: old auto tire
        strong rope, 15′ to 20′

Did you ever see an auto tire swing hanging from a tree? A familiar sight in our country, it is probably the easiest piece of outdoor equipment to make. All you need is an auto tire, a rope and a sturdy branch of a tree.

Get a big person to help you loop the rope around the branch and tie it firmly. Then tie the other end to the tire. It will afford many hours of pleasant relaxation for children as well as grownups.

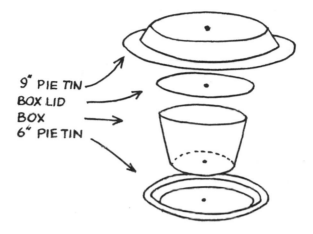

9" PIE TIN
BOX LID
BOX
6" PIE TIN

Come-Hither Bird Feeder

Scrap: cottage cheese container (paper)
two tin-foil plates, 9" and 6"
wire coat hanger
string

Your feathered friends will be grateful to you if you provide them with food this winter.

Next time you finish a carton of cottage cheese wash and dry it, and the lid too. Fill the box with bird seed and put the lid back on. Place a 9" tin-foil plate over the box for a roof, and a 6" tin plate underneath for the floor.

Unbend a wire hanger and poke one end down through the center of the 9" pie plate. Continue through the cover of the cardboard carton, through the carton and out through the bottom plate. Wrap the bottom end of the wire around a nail or twig to keep it from slipping out.

With a pencil poke several holes, the diameter of the

pencil, near the bottom edge of the container. Seeds will fall out onto the bottom plate for the birds to come and feast. Loop the top of the wire so you can tie a string to it and hang your Come-Hither Bird Feeder from the branch of a tree.

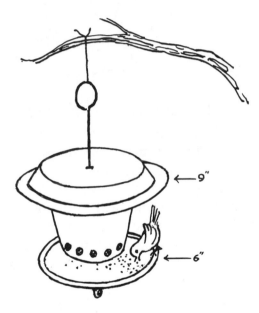

CANDLES
INSIDE
← CAN

Camper's Light

Scrap: large juice can
Other materials: 2 candles
              2 sticks

Remove both ends of a large juice can smoothly and turn the can on its side. Punch several holes with a hammer and nail according to the illustration. They are air holes for the heat of your candles to escape upward, so the candles will burn with steady flames.

Opposite the little holes flatten the tin with a hammer at the places where you will set the candles. Hollow out places in the middle of the two sticks so that you can rest the can there safely with no danger of its rolling off.

Drip a little wax on the flat places and quickly place the candles firmly upright. Put your Camper's Light on a table or inside a tent and it will give you a good amount of illumination.

Fruity Bird Feeder

Scrap: $\frac{1}{2}$ grapefruit rind
 bacon grease
 string

You can be a friend to wild birds who have trouble finding food when the ground is frozen.

After you have finished eating a half grapefruit, clean out all the pulp. Poke a small hole through each side of the grapefruit rind near the top.

Use this grapefruit rind to dispose of bacon grease. When it is about half full, pull the string through the holes and hang the Fruity Bird Feeder over a low branch. It will attract the birds that are suet eaters such as bluebirds, bluejays and chickadees.

Outdoor Barbecue Grill

Scrap: 2 or 4 concrete blocks
          chicken wire or heavier wire

You can make a very handsome, modern-looking grill with concrete blocks and chicken wire. You'll be surprised at how simple it is to make.

Place the concrete blocks on a level area of ground, about 2 feet apart. If the blocks are large enough you will only need two altogether, but otherwise you will need two on each side. Place the chicken wire under the bottom block at (A) so that it won't slip. Pull the wire up, over the top and down the other side, and anchor it below the bottom block at (B).

If you use very heavy wire, all you have to do is lay it across the concrete blocks. The wire should be about 8″ above the top of the fire. You may want a brick base for your fireplace area if you have some scrap bricks. This will give you a little elevation and it will be drier than the ground.

A   B

Decorative Lantern

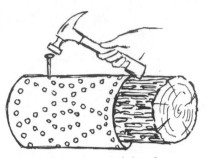

Scrap: large tin can
        8″ piece of wire
        small log
Other material: candle

Draw a design on a piece of paper with dots to represent the spots of light you will want on your lantern. The more dots you draw, the more illumination you will have later.

Tape the paper around the can and find a small log that will fit inside the can. This will keep the can from denting as you hammer a hole at each dot with a sharp nail. Be sure that the log is under the nail as you work. After you have hammered all the dots, make a hole at each side at the top for the handle.

Attach the wire handle through the special holes. Be sure the handle is long enough so your hand won't be too near the candle. Place the candle upright in the bottom of the can, after melting down the bottom of the candle so it will stick.

The Decorative Lantern is finished and ready to cast interesting rays of light.

6.
Creating
Things
to Wear

A   B

Yarn Lapel Dolls

Scrap: yarn
safety pin

Yarn dolls are easy to create and make good gifts for your friends. Wrap yarn around a piece of stiff cardboard or folded paper about 4″ square. Keep wrapping until the yarn is about $\frac{1}{4}$″ thick. Tie the top with a small piece of yarn and cut the bottom open. Remove the cardboard.

About an inch down from the knot at the top, tie another piece of yarn to form the head and neck. Now shape the doll by cutting strands on each side for the arms. Cut some strands for a skirt, but remember to leave enough long strands to make legs.

Tie yarn around the waist and your girl doll is almost complete. Braid the arms and legs and tie small pieces of yarn at the wrists and ankles so they won't unravel.

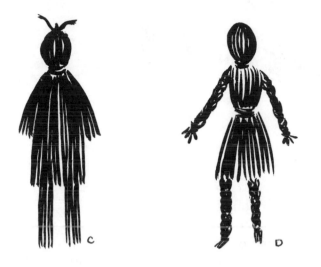

Attach a safety pin to the back and pin the doll to your lapel, hat or beanie.

To make a boy doll, use all the yarn below the waist for legs. Don't cut away any for a skirt. Just divide the yarn and braid it and tie ankles.

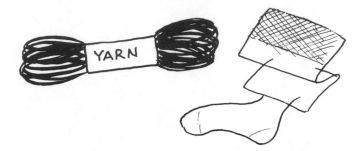

Make a Wig

Scrap: old nylon stockings
skeins of yarn—yellow, black, red, gray, orange or brown

Here is your chance to have long braids, curls or a heavy mane of any color hair you want. Pull the top of a nylon stocking over your head so it fits like a skull cap just above your eyebrows and ears. Knot the rest of the stocking so the knot is close to your head. Cut off the part of the stocking beyond the knot.

Remove the skull cap and put it across a small mixing bowl with the nylon stretched tightly over the open top of the bowl. It is easier to sew this way. First sew the knot so that it stays closed. Then take several skeins of yarn about 36″ long and center them over the nylon skull cap so that yarn hangs down the same amount on

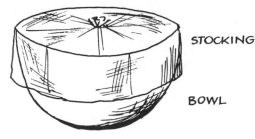

STOCKING

BOWL

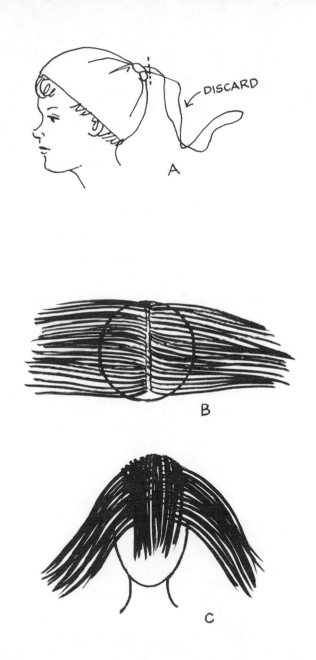

DISCARD

A

B

C

each side. Sew the skeins to the nylon at the "part." This takes care of the sides.

For back "hair" lay more skeins from front to back with shorter ends at the front. These will be bangs. Trim them after you sew the yarn to the skull cap. You can braid your long hair or wear it in a pony tail.

You can make boys' wigs the same way with shorter skeins of yarn. You will get a droll effect by putting the wig on and then placing a pot or a deep bowl over it and trimming the yarn around it.

There are many variations and things you can do with a wig. Have fun experimenting with different colors and different hair styles.

Paper-Bead Necklace

Scrap: color pictures from magazines
Other materials: paste
        shellac
        toothpick

It is amazing what lovely beads you can make from colored magazine pictures. Select pictures that are brightly colored. (The colored comic section is especially good for this project.) Cut about 30 triangles (isosceles) in which two sides are of equal length, and longer than the base line, as shown in the drawing. The width of the base line determines the width of the bead; the length makes your bead thicker or thinner.

Now you have to roll the triangles into beads. Turn the colored side face down. Place a toothpick on the bottom of the triangle and roll the paper around it,

ROLL UP

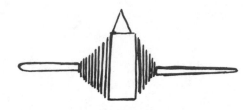

rolling towards the thinner part of the triangle. When you get to the end apply a little paste to the point so it sticks firmly. Shellac each bead as you finish it so the paper holds together better and also gets a nice shiny finish. Remove the toothpick from the bead and start another one while the first bead is drying.

When they are all dry, string them on a sturdy necklace string. Vary your beads in size, two larger beads and one smaller one, and then repeat. You can make very interesting arrangements. You can distribute macaroni or seeds among the beads. It will be hard for anyone to tell that your beads are only made of paper.

Lazy-Day Scuffs

Scrap: leather or felt from old handbag or hat
Other materials: cardboard
        heavy needle and thread

Make a pair of scuffs to laze around the house in. First stand on a piece of cardboard in your stockinged feet. With a crayon draw outlines of your feet. Cut out the patterns.

Cut out leather or felt soles according to the patterns, and also two 2″ bands to fit over your instep. With a heavy needle and strong thread sew the instep band to the sole. Now take the cardboard patterns and use them as inner soles. Glue them to the inside of the soles. If you wish, you can first cover the inner sole with leather, felt or cloth.

Embroider your initials or a little design on the instep, covering with brightly colored yarn to decorate your Lazy-Day Scuffs.

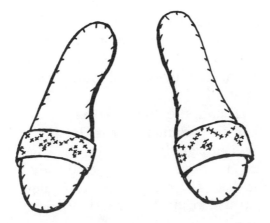

A Beanie

Scrap: old fedora hat

assorted pins and buttons

Here's a good use for that old fedora hat lying about in the attic or closet. Your mother will be glad if you make it into a beanie. Push the fold up to give the hat a rounded top. Then remove the leather band between the brim and the crown of the hat.

Cut off the brim and band with a pair of scissors. Try the hat on. Pull it all the way down. Put your finger under the hat to where your hairline begins. Then make a mark on the outside of the beanie at the same place. Look in the mirror so you will know just how much of the hat to cut off.

Cut all around the hat, so that it is much more shallow than the original crown. It should look like a beanie now. Cut zig-zag all around the edge. If you care to, you can cut circles or triangles or any other shapes out of the hat. If you pin on campaign buttons or badges, you will really look sharp.

Watermelon Seed Necklace

Scrap: watermelon seeds
       string

Watermelon seeds make interesting necklaces. They do not have to be painted because their natural brown is a warm, attractive color. Wash the seeds before you begin to work with them. Spread them out to dry on absorbent paper.

Thread a needle with strong thread. Then pierce your needle through the seeds, one at a time. When your necklace is long enough, knot the ends of the thread together.

When the seeds are still soft and fresh they are easy to string. If you wait until they get brittle they will break as you push your needle through, so remember to use them as soon as they're dry.

Rumpl-Stilt-Can

Scrap: 2 large (46-ounce) fruit juice cans
2 old leather skate straps or belts

You can grow almost a foot taller in just a few minutes if you make yourself these stilts. Remove one end of each can smoothly and punch holes on opposite sides of the other ends. Put the straps through the holes and strap them onto your feet. If you use belts, you will have to punch holes at the right place so the straps will fit snugly. Cut off the extra ends so you won't trip.

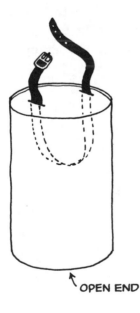

OPEN END

7.
Creating
Musical
Toys

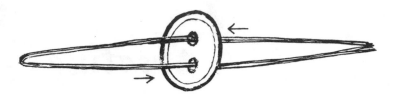

Hummer Toy

Scrap: large button with two holes
5′ of string

This toy comes out of American folklore and is an all-time favorite with many families.

Insert the string through one hole of the button and then thread it through the other button hole in the opposite direction.

Tie the ends together. Push the button to the middle of the string. Place your middle finger of each hand through one end of the loop of string. With hands apart and the string somewhat taut, circle the button 15 or 20 times, twisting the string. Now, while still holding the ends of the string, move your hands slowly together, then away. The button will hum as it speeds around. Keep moving your hands together and apart and the hum will continue.

Inner-Tube Tom-Tom

Scrap: old inner tube
#10 can
heavy bootlace, leather thong or strong twine

Here is a durable tom-tom with a resonant sound. You can make it out of a can and an old inner tube.

Remove both ends of the can smoothly. Cut a 20″ section of inner tube open so that it lies flat. Stand the can on the rubber and measure off two circles about 4″ larger than the diameter of the can. Punch 30 holes around each rubber circle $\frac{1}{2}$″ from the edge. Use a leather punch or an ice pick, and punch them at regular intervals.

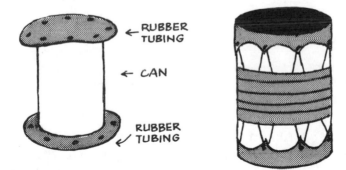

RUBBER TUBING

← CAN

RUBBER TUBING

Cover each end of the can with a circle and lace them together with a leather thong or strong twine. Pull the laces tight, because the tighter you make the lacing, the more resonant the tone will be.

From the rest of the inner tube cut six circular bands each $1\frac{1}{2}$″ wide. Slip them over the can and arrange them so they overlap each other. This helps to hold the drum heads in place, and also makes for a more pleasing tone. Now you are ready to beat out a rhythm.

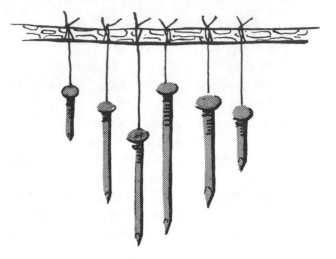

Nail Music

Scrap: 6 or 7 nails of different lengths
      thread
      12″ length of wood

Here's a tinkling rhythm instrument made with nails! Take 6 or 7 nails of different lengths. Tie them to a 12″ length of wood with threads of different lengths.

Now tap each nail with another, extra nail. It will sound like chimes!

Bottle Band

Scrap: 8 or more bottles

Do you have empty bottles lying around the basement or garage? You can make music with them. You will need 8 bottles to correspond to the 8 notes in a musical scale.

If your bottles are the same size and shape your job will be easier. If they vary, try to have them as nearly alike as possible. Wash them if they are dirty.

Line up your 8 bottles on a table. Pour a little water in the bottle farthest to the right. Pour a trifle more water in the bottle next to it. Then still more in the next one, and so on, until each bottle has a little more than its neighbor to the right.

Now the work and fun begins. Tap each bottle with a spoon. You will find each bottle has a tone of its own. The more water in a bottle the lower the tone will be. So to get the tones to sound like the notes in a scale

you will have to add or remove water from some bottles and then test them again. Be prepared to do this many times.

If you have a piano, it will help to play the scale on it. Then tap your bottles and see if you can get the same tones on them. After you have perfected your bottle scale, try to play a tune on it by tapping the right bottles with a spoon.

With more bottles you can set up several scales, and you and your friends can have a real band. Try it. It's fun!

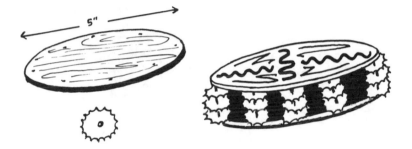

Tambourines

Scrap: 32 pop bottle caps
       two 5″ squares of thin plywood
Other materials: paint
         eight 1″ nails

Tambourines are fine rhythm instruments for rhythm bands, jam sessions or folk dancing. They're fun to make, especially if you like to hammer and bang.

Remove the cork lining from each bottle cap. Flatten the caps with a hammer. With a large nail, punch a hole through each cap.

Cut two circles 5″ in diameter out of plywood. Smooth down the rough edges with sandpaper. Paint one side of each disc and set aside to dry. Then make 8 dots in a circle 1″ in from the edge of one disc. Hammer a 1″ nail completely through each dot.

Place the disc on a flat surface with the nails pointing up. On each nail place 4 flattened bottle caps. Then place the other disc directly on top of the nail ends. Hammer gently into place so that the sharp points of the nails do not go all the way through the wood. Tap your tambourine for a pleasant jingling sound.

Maracas

Scrap: small tin box with tight cover, such as an
    empty typewriter ribbon box
Other materials: dried beans, seeds, sand, pebbles,
    rice, lentils, etc.

Making this interesting rhythm instrument is almost
as much fun as using it. Place a few pellets in the tin
box, close the lid and shake the box. How does it sound?
Experiment with the different materials suggested above
until you hear a sound that pleases you. You can mix
different types of pellets together to vary the effects.

If you want a fine rain rattle, try using rice. Or if
you want the sound of hailstones, use small pebbles.
Sand will give you a soft, slushing sound.

When you have the right pellets, seal the box with a
strip of cellophane or adhesive tape and paint it with
enamel.

8.
Creating
Decorations

Stone Animals

Scrap: small stones
Other materials: cement or glue
            paint

For this creation you may have to go out to look for your materials, but you should be able to find stones easily in your yard or a vacant lot.

First decide what animal you want to make. If it's a turtle, for example, look for an oval-shaped stone about 3 or 4 inches in diameter. Try to find a stone which looks like the body of a turtle. Then look for 4 small stones which resemble the feet of a turtle. They should be of a similar color or tone.

Clean any dirt off the stones. Glue the small foot stones under the large body stone as in the sketch. Use a fifth small stone for the head. Glue that down. Paint in the eyes, nose and mouth. Bolster the head with a piece of wood or stone underneath until the glue dries.

Let it dry overnight. Your animal is ready for display.

You may find other stones that by their very shape will suggest animals to you. Make use of them and just add the necessary details.

Sponge Painting

Scrap: kitchen sponge
Other materials: paint
　　　　　　　　 construction paper

Save those worn-out kitchen sponges! Their texture makes them interesting to paint with. Clean and dry a sponge and then soak it lightly in water color or enamel paint. Squeeze out the excess paint.

Press the sponge lightly on paper to make imprints. Place the prints in an overall design. You may want to plan your design first and mark it in pencil. If you have several sponges, use one for each color. You can overlap the sponge prints or leave space in between.

Paint familiar objects such as animals, houses or boats to hang on the wall. Or paint free abstract forms and designs and use the paper to line your desk drawer after the paint dries.

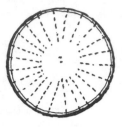

Tin-Foil Flowers

Scrap: tin-foil pie plates and frozen food dishes

You can make a silvery flower garden from tin-foil pie plates and dishes. Small pot-pie tins are especially easy to work with, since they are already round and easy to cut and shape. To make a flower head, cut slits from the edge almost to the center, leaving a circle about the size of a half-dollar. Curl each strip to give the flower a fringed effect. Make stems from the outer reinforced rims of larger pans. Cut the flat parts of these larger pans into leaf shapes.

Make two little holes in the head of the flower and poke one end of a stem in one hole and out the other to attach the flower. Twist one end of a leaf around the stem and you have a complete flower.

Make many different kinds of flowers. You can double some of them by using two pie plates. You can twist the petals into different shapes, and cut them in different sizes. When you have enough flowers, cover a small can with foil. Fill it with sand and place your flowers in it for a silvery bouquet.

Eggshell Mosaics

Scrap: Easter eggshells
Other materials: clear glue
       paper plates

Here is a good way to use the shells from pretty Easter eggs. Or you can dye hard-boiled eggs with various colors. Take the shells off the eggs when the dye is dry and make separate piles of the different colors.

Draw designs on your paper plates. They can be simple, like a bull's eye, or fancy criss-cross designs or flowers or fruits. Spread a thin layer of glue over the plate. Now take pieces of eggshell and place them on the plate to fill out your design. Start from the center of the plate and work towards the edge. It is best to do one color at a time.

Crayon Painting

Scrap: left-over crayons

A very creative use for old crayon stubs is to paint with them! The first thing you do is remove the paper from your pieces of crayon. Then on a piece of drawing or construction paper draw an outline of the objects or design you want to paint.

Spread newspapers over your table and light a sturdy candle. Now you are ready for your painting. Carefully put the tip of the crayon into the flame, and as soon as the wax begins to melt, drip and press with it on your paper. Have several colors of crayons handy so you can apply them to your drawing. Mix your colors by painting one color over the other. The effect is very interesting and closely resembles a thick oil painting.

String Sculpture

Scrap: 20' of string or yarn
Other materials: flour or wallpaper paste
     toy balloon

Inflate the balloon and tie the end securely. Soak your string in a bowl or bucket of wallpaper paste until it is thoroughly wet. Wipe off the surplus with a rag.

Now wind the sticky string or yarn around the inflated balloon. Try to create a decorative design. As you wind the string, triangles, squares and rectangles will form. Do your best to make an interesting maze. When the design satisfies you, stop.

Hang the object up to dry overnight. The string should be stiff by morning. Puncture the balloon and carefully remove it by pulling it out through one of the openings in the sculpture. Hang your work of art from the ceiling with string. Your friends will all admire it.

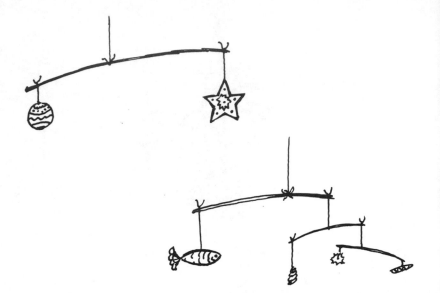

Mobiles

Scrap: 5 sticks of wood about 12″ long
      wire and thread
      odds and ends such as seashells, corks, etc.

A mobile is a free-hanging form of sculpture with movable parts that turn in the slightest current of air.

Start by taking two objects that balance each other in weight and attach them with thread to the ends of a thin stick. This is the simplest form of a mobile. Now you can add to it and make the mobile more intriguing.

Use any scrap materials you wish. Instead of wood sticks, you can try wire. It is fun, but not too easy, to balance objects with each other on the same stick or strut.

Wire Sculpture

Scrap: wire hangers
          or any other flexible wire

Wire can be transformed into very interesting bits of sculpture. If you have strong fingers, you can use wire coat hangers; otherwise, use thinner, more flexible wire.

Animals are fun to make. Take a piece of wire and wind it around a pencil to make a coil. Make four coils and you will have four legs for your dog sculpture. Now twist another piece of wire connecting the four pieces to make the body and head of the dog.

Here are other ideas:

Bend wire to make a skyscraper. Draw the outlines of windows on paper and paste them to the wire framework.

Twist a piece of wire so that it resembles the shape of a bird. Make two legs with coils (as in the first project) and connect to the body. Twist each leg at the bottom into a circle so that the bird will be able to stand up.

It will take a little practice in working with wire but you will find it fascinating. If the wire is not flexible enough, you can use pliers or tin snips.

You may want to make free abstract designs that you can hang from the ceiling with a string. You can add other scrap articles such as cork, spools, buttons to give your sculpture more variety.

9. Creating Toys and Games

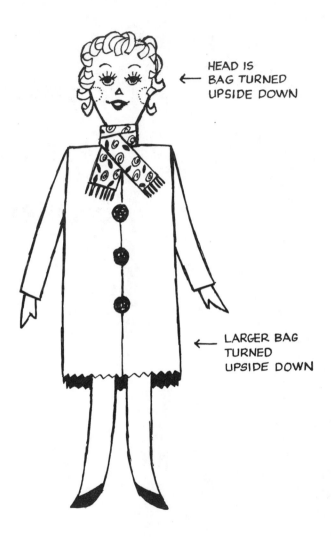

HEAD IS
← BAG TURNED
UPSIDE DOWN

LARGER BAG
← TURNED
UPSIDE DOWN

Paper-Bag Puppets

Scrap: 2 paper bags
newspapers
Other materials: crayons or paints
string

You can make a delightful puppet out of two used paper bags. Flatten one bag and turn it upside down. With crayons or paints draw a big face over the entire bag. Crumple up several sheets of newspaper and stuff them in the bag. This is the puppet's head. Tie the end of the bag with a string but leave enough space to push your forefinger into the bag in order to manipulate the head.

Make curls by wrapping strips of paper around a pencil. After you remove the pencil, paste the curled strips to the puppet's head for hair.

The second bag will be the body. Make a small opening in the middle of the closed end of the bag. Take the head and slip the neck through the opening in the body. Cut arms and legs of paper and paste them to the bag. You can cut the bag to resemble pants if your puppet is a boy. Decorate it with bright colors.

Make several characters and put on a play for your friends. All you have to do to work your puppet is to put your arm into the bag and your finger into the head.

Peep Show

Scrap: 2 corrugated cartons 12″ x 24″
Other materials: colored cellophane
        flashlight

There is something fascinating about a peep show, especially one with lights that change color.

First cut two small peep holes on the long side of a carton at (A), and another hole large enough for a flashlight at (B). Now cut a cardboard wheel about 4″ in diameter and cut three 1″ holes in it (C). Paste cellophane of different colors over each hole in the disc.

Push a brad through the center of the disc and attach it to the carton over the large opening so that the flashlight will throw colored light through to the inside of the carton.

Now paint your stage setting on the inside bottom of the other carton. Or you can paste a magazine picture on instead. Slide the second box inside the first box so the scene is opposite the holes. You can produce a scene from "Alice in Wonderland," "Treasure Island," or a play you make up. Use pipe-cleaner figures and make cardboard furniture and paste them all in place. Get your flashlight ready, and you can open your peep show.

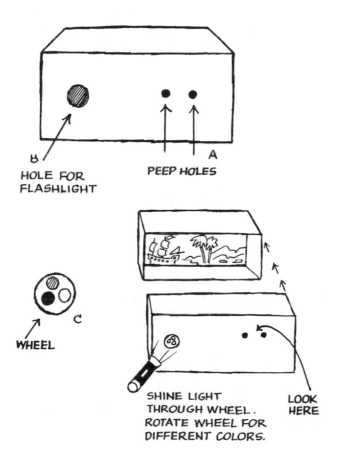

B
HOLE FOR
FLASHLIGHT

PEEP HOLES

A

WHEEL

C

SHINE LIGHT
THROUGH WHEEL.
ROTATE WHEEL FOR
DIFFERENT COLORS.

LOOK
HERE

93

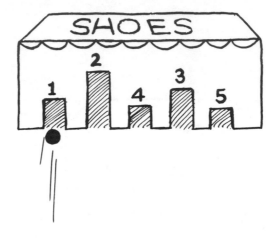

Marble Game

Scrap: cardboard shoe box
Other material: marbles

Turn a shoe box upside down and cut about 5 notches on the long side of the box. The notches should be 1″ wide and in different heights from 2″ to 5″. Write a large number above each hole.

Place the box on the floor against a wall and pace off 5 steps. Give each player 10 marbles and keep score. Players take turns rolling their marbles into the holes, and they score according to the number on top. The first player to get 100 wins.

Pull Train

Scrap: 3 or 4 large corrugated paper cartons
rope
crayons

Just about every child likes to play with empty cartons. Rope several cartons together to make a train. The cartons should be large enough for a small child to sit in.

First make the locomotive. Draw an engine stack on a piece of cardboard and fit it onto the top of a closed carton. You may have to pierce the carton. Draw other familiar parts of a locomotive on the sides of the box.

Draw large train wheels on the other cartons. With scissors, pierce holes in the fronts and backs of the cartons for the rope to go through. Be sure to make large, firm knots at each end of the pieces of rope after you thread them through. You can use the Pull Train indoors or out.

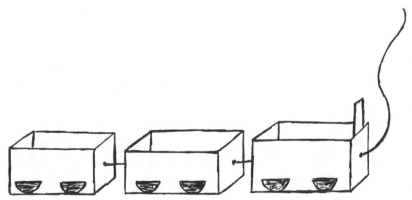

Clothespin Ring Toss

Scrap: cardboard box cover about 16″ square, 2″ deep
Other materials: 6 rubber jar rings
          9 wooden clothespins

Clothespin Ring Toss is a game of skill that you can make very easily. Cut 9 pairs of slits in a cardboard box cover so that you can stand a clothespin firmly in each pair of slits.

Mark the base of each clothespin with a number from 1 to 9. Use a crayon or a felt marker.

To play the game, set a toss line 6′ or more away and try to throw 6 rubber jar rings over the clothespins. Add up your score. You and your friends can take turns and see who gets the best score.

Tops

Scrap: empty spools
      milk bottle caps
      pop bottle caps
      lollipop sticks

It's very easy to make an assortment of tops out of empty spools, caps, and so on. Make them very attractive by decorating them with poster paints.

If you are using an empty wooden spool, paint dots and lines all over it using bright colors. Cut a lollipop stick so that it is only an inch or so longer than the spool. Insert it through the hole of the spool. Keep the pointed end of the stick pointing down since this is the point the top spins on. Paint the stick, too.

For the cardboard milk bottle cap you will have to punch a hole directly in the center. If it is off-center, the top will be wobbly. Insert your lollipop stick through the hole. If the pointed end is not sharp enough you can trim it with a knife or pencil sharpener. Decorate your top.

When your tops spin, notice how the colors blend with each other and seem to change.

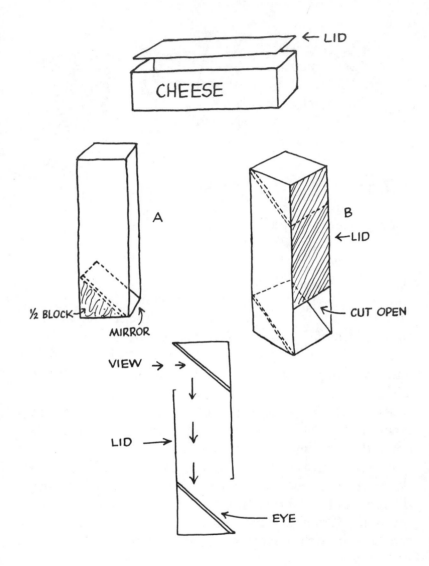

LID

CHEESE

A

B

½ BLOCK

MIRROR

LID

CUT OPEN

VIEW

LID

EYE

Periscope

Scrap: long wooden cheese box and lid
      or paper box
      2 small mirrors from old pocketbooks
      block of wood about 2″ x 2″ x 2″

Make a periscope that you can really use from an empty cheese box! Remove the cover but save it. Saw the block of wood in half diagonally. Glue one half of the block into one corner of the box and glue the mirror to it so the mirror rests at a 45-degree angle.

Now cut 2″ off one end of the lid and put it back on. Glue it if necessary to keep it in place.

Turn the box around and cut away a 2″ section of the bottom of the box at the opposite end from the mirror. Now glue the other half of the block into place and glue the second mirror to it. This mirror will face in the opposite direction from the first mirror.

Your periscope is now ready to use.

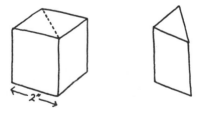

Punching Bag

Scrap: flour or meal sack made of cloth
         rags

Don't let your mother throw away the cloth sack that flour or meal came in. You can put it to good use if you want to make a punching bag.

Stuff a large sack with rags until the sack is very hard. Then tie the top closed with a strong piece of twine. Leave two ends about 4" long. Tie these ends of twine to a low beam, a clothesline or anything handy so that the punching bag hangs as high as your shoulder. Then you can practice punching every time you feel like it.

Walnut Jump-ups

Scrap: empty walnut shells

Next time you crack walnuts try to open them at the seam so you don't break the shells. You can make little walnut jump-ups to amuse some of your younger friends.

Take two half shells. Paste a little paper hinge to the inside of both shells so they are connected. Now draw a little jump-up figure on some stiff paper. Color it, cut it out, and fold it like an accordion. Paste the bottom of the figure inside the bottom shell.

Fold the figure all the way down. Then close the top shell. Offer the nut to one of your friends.

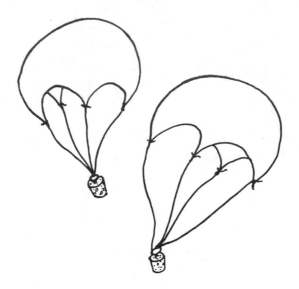

Parachute

Scrap: large rag or old handkerchief
       corks
       string

Cut a large rag into a 12″ square. Then cut 4 strings into 12″ lengths. Tie each string to a corner of the cloth. Tie the 4 strings together at the end and tack them to a cork.

From a height toss you parachute into the air and it will float down slowly like a real parachute. If you use the parachute outdoors, tie a stone or some heavy object to the four strings so the parachute will descend more quickly. You can make many parachutes of different sizes and let them descend together like a parachute patrol.

Water Scooter

Scrap: lid of a wooden cigar box
        rubber band

Draw a boat on your piece of wood as nearly like the one in the drawing as possible. Carefully cut it with a coping saw. Out of the rest of the wood cut a small paddle wheel.

Stretch your rubber band across the notches. Put the paddle wheel between the strands of the rubber band and twist it. Keep twisting until it is wound up, and then put the boat in a bathtub of water or a little pond and let it go. You will be amazed at how well it will scoot through the water.

If you have extra pieces of wood, make several boats and paint them different colors. You can have boat races with your friends.

Toothpick Holder

Scrap: 3 large wooden spools
       left-over yarn, string or ribbon

You can make a holder for toothpicks or large darning needles out of empty spools. Place three spools together so they form a triangle, two spools side by side, and the third one in front. Now take strands of left-over wool or string and wrap them around the three spools. Cover the spools from top to bottom. Be sure to pull the yarn tightly.

When you have finished, tie the wool or string so it will not unravel. Glue three little circles of paper over the holes in the bottoms of the spools. Now you have a holder for toothpicks or darning needles.

Animal Bean Bags

Scrap: pieces of cloth, buttons
Other materials: dried beans or gravel

Draw an animal form about 6″ long on a piece of paper. It can be a fish, dog or any other animal you prefer. Cut out your figure to use as a pattern.

Fold the cloth double and place your pattern on it. Pin the pattern to the cloth and cut around it. Now you are ready to sew the two pieces of cloth together.

If you know how to use a sewing machine, your job will be much quicker and easier. However, you can also sew your bean bag by hand. If your cloth is printed on one side only, turn this inside to sew, and afterwards turn it right-side out. However, if you want to use overcast or blanket stitches, keep the printed sides on the outside.

Sew almost all the way around, but leave a little place open to pour in the dried beans or gravel. After that, sew up the opening with the same stitches. Then sew on buttons for the eyes, and embroider other details such as wings, fins, mouth, and so on.

Cork Soldier

Scrap: 2 large corks
2 medium corks
12 small corks
pieces of wire, or pipe cleaners

A cork soldier is a favorite toy for little boys to play with. You can make a really nice one out of corks.

First pierce each cork through the center with an ice pick, or with a hammer and long nail. This will take a little time, and you must be careful not to hurt yourself. Use pieces of flexible wire or pipe cleaners to connect the corks. Turn the ends of the wires so that the corks won't slip off.

Try the various corks in different ways to make a soldier who really looks like somebody. Try medium-size corks for the head and hat, large corks for the waist and body, and small corks for the arms and legs. Experiment with the wire too. You can make it tight or loose. When you like the way your soldier shapes up, paint on his face and uniform.

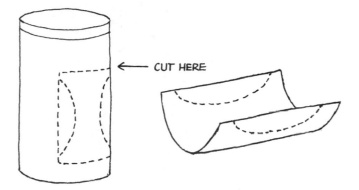

← CUT HERE

Doll Cradle

Scrap: cylindrical cereal box

You can amuse your little sister by making a cradle for one of her small dolls. All you need is a cylindrical box such as oatmeal or cornmeal come in. Paste on the lid so it won't come off. Then with a pencil mark lines like the dotted lines in the drawing.

Use scissors to cut along the lines. The wider part will be the canopy over the doll's head, and the other end is the foot of the cradle. From the piece you cut out make rockers. Make slits across the bottom of the cradle and push in the rockers. Decorate the cradle with colored paper or crayon designs.

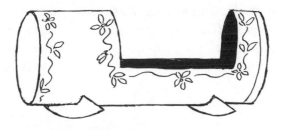

Paper-Plate Hat

Scrap: paper plates
colored paper
straws, pine cones, pipe cleaners, buttons, paper cups, small empty plastic bottles and other miscellaneous scrap

Other material: glue

Everyone loves to make a hat, particularly a silly hat. Take a paper plate and try to create the most interesting hat you can out of the assortment of miscellaneous scrap.

Try to make something intriguing. You might glue a paper cup to the plate and poke a colorful pipe stem through the cup. You might also poke pencils through the sides and have a little bottle with a few flowers in it.

Use any of the materials available and try to make your hat very zany.

Keep your hat from falling off your head by punching a hole on each side of the plate to pull a ribbon or string through. Tie the ends under your chin.

This is also good to do at a party. Give each child a paper plate and a few odds and ends to work with.

Freshy . . . The Puppet

Scrap: plain paper bag

Freshy is a puppet who deserves his name. He sticks his tongue out at his audience and can even touch his nose with his tongue if he's coaxed hard enough.

Draw Freshy's round face on a paper bag. Then put

in his eyes, mouth, nose and hair, and give him a few freckles over his nose. Cut out a circle large enough for your thumb at his mouth, and another at his nose.

Put the bag over your hand and stick your index finger out of the nose and stick your thumb out for the tongue. You can color your thumb red with crayon to make it look more like a tongue. Talk to Freshy and give him a chance to reply by wiggling his nose and sticking out his tongue.

10.
Sickbed
Fun

Lapboard

Scrap: corrugated carton about 16″ x 20″
        empty shoe box
        wallpaper or magazine pictures
Other materials: glue or tape

If you or any other member of your family is sick, you will find a Lapboard very useful.

First cut off the flaps of the carton. Trim off the top edge so the carton is about 8″ or 10″ high. Cut away a rectangular section from both the long sides of the carton to fit over your lap.

Next glue or tape the shoe box to one side of the

carton. It can hold games, pencils or hankies. Decorate the top and sides of the carton with wallpaper or magazine pictures.

A sick person will enjoy using the Lapboard for games, food or writing.

Scrap Collage

Scrap: a variety of objects such as buttons, paper clips, travel postcards, cancelled stamps, etc.

A Scrap Collage is a design created by pasting or attaching a number of assorted items onto a background. You can tell a story through the items you use for your collage or you can create a design that is just interesting to look at.

Suppose you want your collage to tell the story of an interesting experience, such as a trip to Canada. You could use the menu of a French restaurant where you ate, the ticket stubs from a play that you saw, a picture postcard, and so on.

Arrange your items in a design on a heavy paper background and paste them in place. Connect them with colored string or yarn threaded with paper clips or buttons if you want to. You can paint designs or pictures on as well, or simply color the background in appropriate tones.

Overlap and arrange your scrap items spontaneously. Making a collage should be a very free type of art work, so don't limit yourself. It's fun to use your little scrap items this way.

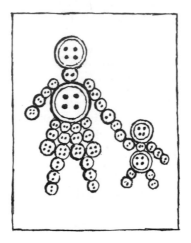

Button Pictures

Scrap: old buttons
Other materials: paste
                construction paper

Almost every home has buttons which no one needs any more. Here's an idea of how to use them and have fun.

First arrange the buttons to form men or horses or a flower garden or a pretty design, on top of the paper. When you are satisfied with your picture, paste each button onto the paper. Or you can sew them down with needle and thread.

Another way to make interesting Button Pictures is to paste them onto magazine pictures for added decoration.

11. Artcraft Work

Papier Mâché Bowls

Scrap: old newspapers
Other materials: library paste
        petroleum jelly
        poster colors
        shellac

You can create many things out of papier mâché. Here are some bowls that are easy and fun to make.

Tear up about 30 sheets of old newspapers into inch-sized bits. Put them in an old pail and pour in enough water to cover all the paper. Stir it around so all the pieces get wet. Let this mixture stand for two days. If the paper seems dry when you inspect it, add some more water.

After about two days drain off the excess water if there is any, and add about 3 tablespoons of paste. Mix thoroughly with your hands until the paper begins to feel like soft clay. It is now papier mâché.

Find a bowl with a pleasing shape that you would like to copy. Turn it upside down and cover it with petroleum jelly. Then apply a $\frac{1}{2}''$ layer of papier mâché. Cover it completely and smoothly. Wait until it is almost dry and then carefully lift it away from the bowl. Let it stand in a safe place until it is completely dried.

If the surface seems rough, sandpaper it smooth and then paint it with bright poster paints. You can decorate it to look like a Mexican bowl! Shellac it afterwards for a glazed finish.

Spatter-Paint Book Covers

Scrap: old toothbrush
Other materials: water color paints
             wrapping paper
             leaf, flat flower, fern or other object

Cut a piece of wrapping paper large enough to cover your favorite book. On the part that will cover the front of the book, place a leaf or other flat object with a nice shape.

Dip the toothbrush into a cup of water color, shake off the surplus paint, and you are ready to spatter-paint a decoration. Scrape a piece of cardboard against the toothbrush so that the paint spatters over the leaf and around it. Don't move the leaf until you have a nice heavy coat of spatters all around it. The leaf will form an outline or silhouette.

Now you can cover your book with a pretty cover that will keep the binding clean.

Marbleized Paper

Scrap: left-over cans of house paint
   paper

Marbleized paper looks exactly like real marble. It has lovely swirling designs and is quite beautiful. It is fun to make but rather messy, so try to work carefully. Spread newspapers on the table or floor before you begin, and wear an apron over your clothes.

Fill a large, shallow pan with about 2 inches of water. Wait for the water to be still. Then sprinkle the water with a few drops of oil paints. Be sure to use different colors for a rich effect. Wait for the drops to rise up to the surface of the water.

Then with an old pencil or stick, swirl the paints a little as you would swirl finger paints. When it is still again, take a sheet of paper and carefully place it on the oiled surface of the water. Lift a corner to see if the marbleizing is taking effect. As soon as you see it adhering to the paper remove the paper and put it on some newspapers to dry. Be sure to have the marbleized side facing up. You can use this paper for gift wrappings, book covers, or for lining shelves and drawers.

Window-Shade Art

Scrap: worn window shade
Other material: enamel paint

Perhaps you have a shabby window shade that still works. You can decorate it and at the same time cover the worn parts and little holes.

Spread out your window shade over newspapers on the floor or on a table, and weight the ends so it stays flat. Over the entire shade, paint a scene or a design that covers every part. Be sure that the paint fills in the worn parts and the cracks and holes. Let the paint dry overnight and then hang your shade in your window.

Index